the
Weekend®
Crafter

Dried Flower
Crafting

the
Weekend®
Crafter

Dried Flower Crafting

20 Easy & Elegant Projects for Your Home

VALERIE SHRADER

LARK BOOKS
A Division of Sterling Publishing Co., Inc.
New York

To my grandmothers,
Edith Roberts Garrison
and
Pauline Gerard Van Arsdale,
who both loved flowers.
I am grateful for their stories of violets
and their gifts of gardenias.

ART DIRECTOR:
CELIA NARANJO

WITH ASSISTANCE FROM:
TOM METCALF

COVER DESIGN:
BARBARA ZARETSKY

PHOTOGRAPHY:
KEITHWRIGHT.COM

ILLUSTRATIONS:
ORRIN LUNDGREN

EDITORIAL ASSISTANCE:
DELORES GOSNELL

ART ASSISTANT:
SHANNON YOKELEY

ART INTERN:
LORELEI BUCKLEY

Library of Congress Cataloging-in-Publication Data

Shrader, Valerie Van Arsdale.
    Dried flower crafting : 20 easy & elegant projects for your home / by Valerie Van Arsdale Shrader.
        p. cm. — (The Weekend crafter)
    ISBN 1-57990-363-0 (paper)
    1. Nature craft. 2. Dried flowers. I. Title. II. Series.

TT157 .S523 2002
745.5—dc21   2002073998

10 9 8 7 6 5 4 3 2 1

First Edition

Published by Lark Books, a division of
Sterling Publishing Co., Inc.
387 Park Avenue South, New York, N.Y. 10016

© 2003, Lark Books

Distributed in Canada by Sterling Publishing,
c/o Canadian Manda Group, One Atlantic Ave., Suite 105
Toronto, Ontario, Canada M6K 3E7

Distributed in the U.K. by Guild of Master Craftsman Publications Ltd., Castle Place,
166 High Street, Lewes, East Sussex, England
BN7 1XU
Tel: (+ 44) 1273 477374, Fax: (+ 44) 1273 478606, Email: pubs@thegmcgroup.com,
Web: www.gmcpublications.com

Distributed in Australia by Capricorn Link (Australia) Pty Ltd.,
P.O. Box 704, Windsor, NSW 2756 Australia

The written instructions, photographs, designs, patterns, and projects in this volume are intended for the personal use of the reader and may be reproduced for that purpose only. Any other use, especially commercial use, is forbidden under law without written permission of the copyright holder.

Every effort has been made to ensure that all the information in this book is accurate. However, due to differing conditions, tools, and individual skills, the publisher cannot be responsible for any injuries, losses, and other damages that may result from the use of the information in this book.

If you have questions or comments about this book, please contact:
Lark Books
67 Broadway
Asheville, NC 28801
(828) 253-0467
Printed in the USA

ISBN 1-57990-363-0

CONTENTS

INTRODUCTION 6

PRESERVATION METHODS 8

TOOLS AND TECHNIQUES....................................16

PROJECTS

    Drawer Pulls 24

    Translucent Lamp 26

    Floral Spheres 28

    Blooming Gift Bags 30

    Kitchen Trellis 33

    Decorated Lampshade 35

    Tonal Arrangement....................................37

    Compass Shadow Box 39

    Flower Power Collection 42

    Ribbon Sachet Bag 46

    Rose and Moss Boxes 49

    Aromatic Coasters.....................................51

    Wrapped Mirror 53

    New Age Stook 56

    Herbal Guest Baskets 58

    Natural Table Runner 61

    Curtain with Pansy Streamers 63

    Pavé Rose Basket 66

    Wreath Triptych 68

    Sublime Stationery Set 71

    First Blush of Spring Swag 75

TEMPLATES 78

CONTRIBUTING DESIGNERS 80

ACKNOWLEDGMENTS 80

INDEX 80

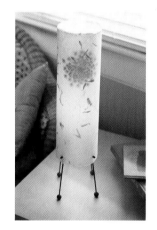

INTRODUCTION

WELCOME TO *Dried Flower Crafting,* a celebration of using dried flowers in new and unique ways. Although it's true that the book includes an arrangement, a swag, and a wreath or two (okay, three), you won't find page after page of flower displays that only a professional floral designer could assemble. Instead, you'll find curtains, cards, candles, lamps, drawer pulls, and other items that include dried and pressed flowers as a central design element. If you can wield a glue gun, hold a paintbrush, or thread a needle, there is a project here for you. No doubt, you'll discover what I have—that preserved flowers are remarkable, versatile, even breathtaking materials that can easily be incorporated into a variety of crafting processes.

If you're intimidated by the thought of working with dried flowers because they're fragile, you may be surprised to discover how resilient they can be; I know, because I've dropped a few! Merely treat them as carefully as you would a delicate sheet of vellum or a fine piece of silk. You certainly can't argue with their exceptional beauty as a crafting element.

You'll also find information in the book for drying and pressing your own flowers, because it's far easier to do than you may have imagined. I've gotten so much pleasure from experimenting with the materials from my own yard that you might want to give it a try, too. The first specimens I preserved in silica gel—a perfect iris and bud—were amazingly vivid. Read over the section on preserving flowers and find a method that appeals to you. You can begin this craft with little or no investment, and it will be with you for a lifetime.

This is much more than a list of preservation methods, though. The heart of the book is indeed the projects, because they enable you to use preserved flowers in delightfully original ways. Several talented designers were inspired by this

notion and created the exciting pieces in this book, like the stationery set on page 71 and the mirror on page 53. Even those that are more traditional in nature, like the wreaths on page 68, have an updated, modern look. Glance over the project section and see how varied the uses of these materials can be; some general crafting skills are all that you'll need to start enjoying this book. And, these are projects that you can complete in a weekend, so you'll be able to explore the possibilities of using dried or pressed flowers quickly and easily.

It's very satisfying to nurture the plants that I later use in projects, and I also love to botanize in the mountains around my home. But most assuredly, you need not be a master gardener or even know much about flowers, for that matter, to create any of the projects in this book. Florists, craft and hobby stores, and even floral departments in large supermarkets stock dried or pressed flowers, so you can readily purchase these materials. There are also a number of vendors with websites, so you can now shop for dried flowers on your home computer if you wish. And, of course, you can buy fresh flowers and dry them yourself. How you obtain your materials isn't as important as how much pleasure they bring you while you work.

Be creative with the projects, too. Blue wreaths don't match your décor? Then investigate the other flowers that are available and find the perfect color for your home. Part of the real fun of working with preserved flowers is the discovery process, finding out how the materials and techniques best complement each other.

So, I encourage you to work with dried or pressed flowers. Walk around your garden, visit your florist, or browse your craft store and find something beautiful. Then, since flowers bring such joy to our lives, take delight in crafting with dried flowers.

PRESERVATION METHODS

LET'S BEGIN by discussing the techniques you can use at home to preserve flowers. There are a number of different procedures you can try, depending on how you plan to craft with the finished product. Some projects may require dried flowers, like the tonal arrangement on page 37, while others need pressed flowers, like the lampshade on page 26. If you want a rustic look, air drying is probably fine; if you want a truly lifelike product, try a desiccant like silica gel. Flower preservation is not an exact science, and there are many variables; often you have to match the process with the flower to achieve the most success, so have some patience as you begin. Here's a basic overview of drying techniques, starting with choosing fresh materials. Remember that you can use the preservation methods with purchased flowers, too.

Here's an assortment of flowers from my yard and garden that were dried or pressed, including iris, flame azalea, peony, daffodil, violet, dogwood, columbine, pansy, Jacob's ladder, and verbena.

CHOOSING FLOWERS

What kind of flowers can you preserve? The possibilities are as varied as nature itself, and even if some varieties don't lend themselves well to pressing, they may dry beautifully. I began looking for plants in my own yard, pressing dogwood and native plants like azalea and columbine. A stroll through local nurseries and garden centers turned up a variety of species to experiment with—verbena, lisianthus, and Gerber daisies, for example.

Practically everyone has let a rose hang to dry, so you probably know that is an excellent method for that species. The traditional everlasting varieties, such as statice and strawflower, are good candidates for this method, but other flowers, like blazing star, larkspur, and delphinium, dry quite nicely when left to hang.

Spring bulbs, such as daffodils, tulips, and irises, dry with amazing realism in silica gel. Annuals like marigolds and zinnias work well in gel, too. Of course, you can get a good idea of which flowers you can use by glancing at the projects in this book.

Every flower has unique qualities that may affect your projects. Even though each of the varieties used in the projects shown in the photo at top right was pressed in the microwave, each behaves a little differently. For example, the marigold petals have to be pressed separately

Each of the flowers shown in the projects here, from left to right, marigold, osteospermum, and daisy, were pressed in the microwave, but each exhibit different characteristics when dried.

and reconstructed. The white osteospermum becomes infused with the purple from the underside of the flower when it is pressed. The daisy dries beautifully but quickly begins to reabsorb moisture, so it must be used (or sealed) immediately after pressing.

You will also find that certain colors or related species react differently to the preservation process. For instance, deep red roses tend to fade to almost black, but the lighter pinks remain lovely. Similarly, certain types of pansies require slightly different drying times; these examples reinforce the importance of keeping a journal or record as you work. If you become passionate about drying your own flowers, you will probably want to study the various species in more depth.

HARVESTING FLOWERS

It's best to harvest flowers late on a sunny morning when the morning dew has evaporated. As the day progresses, especially in the height of the summer, the blooms will wilt from the midday heat, so gather them early when the plant itself is full of moisture, yet not wet. Likewise, you should avoid harvesting after a rain shower, with all the additional moisture that brings. If you absolutely can't avoid picking flowers when they are slightly wet, bring them inside and let them stand in a vase until they are dry.

If you plan to harvest lots of flowers and need to spend some time in the garden, you may want to bring along a container of water. Place the stems inside as you clip them, because you must begin the drying process with fresh blossoms. For just a brief trip, a basket will suffice to hold the blooms, as long as you plan to start working with the material immediately. In general, you should begin the preservation process as quickly as possible after harvesting.

These roses, which are being wired for air drying, are still lovely and fresh. Be sure that all the flowers you choose for drying and pressing are in pristine condition.

Here's some obvious advice: pick only perfect specimens. A flower damaged by insects or disease certainly won't improve during the drying process. Take a few more stems than you think you will need, for insurance against unsatisfactory results. Bear in mind that the flowers may shrink while drying, depending on which method you choose, so you may discover that you need a little more material than you originally anticipated.

A flower's blooming cycle should also be taken into consideration when you're looking for material. You probably don't want a bloom that's been on the stem for a few days, because its beauty is beginning to fade. Look for fresh, unblemished blooms. With some species, you have to time your harvest perfectly, for its bloom may be open only for a day.

Lastly, look out for insects. My peonies always seem to have an ant or two crawling around inside the petals. Remove the bugs before you bring the flowers into the house. An undetected insect can continue to munch on air-dried flowers, so be particularly vigilant if you use this method.

PREPARING FOR PRESERVATION

Generally, the greenery on a flower stem will not dry at the same rate as the bloom, and some stalks just won't dry well at all; you may have a beautiful blossom and an ugly brown stem. But don't be afraid to experiment. I harvested some peonies and kept just a leaf because

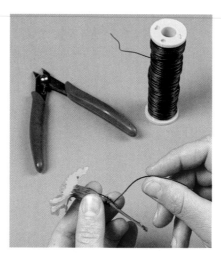

To wire the stems, insert the wire through the calyx and bend down; then, wrap it around several times to form a stem or handle.

it framed the flower so nicely, and indeed it dried beautifully. Most authorities recommend removing all the foliage and stem before drying in silica gel, though there are some exceptions to this rule (some of the spring-flowering bulbs, for instance).

Depending on the intended use of the flowers after they are dried, you may find that it is helpful to wire the stems first, as shown in the photo at center below. This little handle of wire is very handy when you are removing the silica gel and sure helps if you want to seal the flowers afterward; you can insert the wire into floral foam while you spray the blossoms with the sealer. Of course, if you choose to use the microwave, you cannot wire the stem before drying.

DRYING TECHNIQUES

Now that you have prepared your flowers, which method will you choose to preserve them? Each species of flower will react differently to a specific preservation process, some with surprising results. Begin small, with just one or two specimens, to test the process; then see how the flowers dried using that method work within the context of your craft project. Keep a record of your attempts, too. A little time and experimentation can be an investment in success and satisfaction later on.

Compare these peonies: the specimen on the left was dried in silica gel, while the one on the right was left to hang dry.

Air Drying

This is the simplest method of drying—you just sit and wait! There are several different options to choose as you merely let nature take its course.

Hanging is really, really easy. Many perennials, like blazing star and larkspur, dry exceptionally well in this simple process. Roses, too, are well suited to this method. Merely bind the stems together (rubber bands work well) and hang them upside down. It's best to group together only the same type of flower, picked at a similar stage of blooming, since they will have approximately the same drying time. Pick a dry, warm location for drying, preferably out of the bright sunlight. The flowers will retain more of their natural color if they dry in a dark spot. Give them a peek every few days to check their progress.

Screen drying is another easy method. Here, simply spread the blooms on a wire screen and turn them every day or two to prevent curling. The screen allows ample ventilation during the drying cycle. This process works well for single flowers; if you want to dry the stems, too, use a screen with mesh that is wide enough to slip them through, and let the bloom rest flat on the screen.

Some flowers dry quite well in an upright position, too. The daffodils in the swag on page 75 were all dried in this manner; they were placed in a vase and allowed to dry naturally. They tend to better retain the gentle bend below the flower head if they sit upright as they dry. You should cut the stems at an angle and remove all the foliage before you place the flowers in just a bit of water in the vase; then leave them to dry.

Desiccant Drying

Desiccants are substances that absorb the moisture in plants. Sand, borax, cornmeal, and cat litter have been used to dry flowers, but silica gel crystals produce wondrous results. Although it is somewhat pricey, silica gel can be reused again and again, both as a normal drying agent and in the microwave; when it has absorbed all the moisture it can handle, silica gel crystals can be reactivated in the oven. Since the flowers have to be covered completely with the substance, you may need a fair amount to get started, maybe 10 pounds (4.5 kg) or so. But once you see how realistic the results are, you'll probably consider it a wise investment in your hobby.

USING SILICA GEL

To begin drying flowers with silica gel, try the traditional method of covering the flowers with the crystals and letting them sit in a closed container for several days. I've been able to achieve much more reliable results with this method, as opposed to using silica gel in the microwave. But you may love the latter method since it's so quick, so don't let me deter you! Rest assured, I'm not a microwave-basher; flowers press beautifully in the microwave, and this method will be discussed on page 14.

Traditional Silica Gel Method

For this method, start with flowers that are completely dry. Use an airtight container with a tight-fitting lid, like a plastic food storage box. Put about 1 inch (2.5 cm) of crystals in the bottom of the container. Then, remove most of the stem,

Cover the fresh flowers completely with silica gel crystals, using a spoon to carefully sprinkle the crystals over the blooms.

since the majority of the stems won't dry well, as stated previously. Add the flowers, making sure that they don't touch each other. Some blooms, like many of the spring-flowering bulbs and tall flowers on spikes such as larkspur and delphinium, are best dried on their sides; a support of cardboard or other material is helpful to preserve the integrity of the bloom.

After you have placed the flowers in the container, add the silica gel crystals. Pour gently around the flowers first, so the crystals begin to fill in under the petals. Then, you may want to use a spoon to continue the process, as shown in the photo. Lightly sprinkle crystals to cover the flower, yet be careful to retain the shape of the bloom. Completely envelop the flowers with crystals and cover the container.

When will your flowers be dry? Three or four days, probably, but some varieties could take up to a week. After a couple of days, gently pour off some of the crystals and check the blossoms. They should feel dry, crisp and light to the touch, almost like a thin piece of paper. To remove all the silica gel, gently and carefully pour it off into another

Delicately remove the crystals from the dried blossom, using a small paintbrush.

container, making sure not to crush the flowers with a rush of crystals.

After you have uncovered the flowers, you will need to dust off the crystals that may be inside the petals. Holding the stem or wire, delicately shake the flower to remove the crystals. You can use a small paintbrush to brush off any stubborn silica gel, as shown in the photo at center below, but do this cautiously.

Microwave Silica Gel Method

The convenience and quickness of this method may appeal to you, although it will probably take some initial testing to arrive at the proper cooking times for the flowers you're drying. Thoroughly read the manufacturer's instructions before you begin, and be sure to let the gel cool before you remove the flowers.

Keep good records of your adventures with microwave drying. It does involve a little experimentation, partly because ovens vary, but of course flowers do, too. To use this technique, cover the flowers with silica gel as in the traditional method, but remember that you can't wire the stems. Be sure to use a microwave-safe container, and double check the instructions on your silica gel for suggested drying times as well as the power settings for your microwave. Try 50 percent power for two minutes to dry marigolds, for instance, cooking them in one-minute increments. Don't forget—to avoid disappointment, let the crystals cool completely before you remove the flowers.

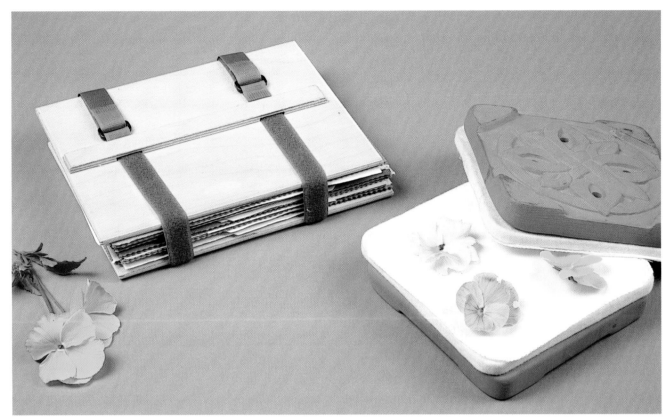

A traditional flower press, on the left, and a microwave press, on the right

PRESSING TECHNIQUES

Pressed flowers can embellish many craft projects because of their two-dimensional nature; they can be glued or decoupaged onto just about anything, with a great deal of success. Like drying, there are several different methods you can utilize to press flowers. While I successfully dried some bleeding heart using the old-fashioned method of placing them in a heavy book, for instance, they did nothing but brown in the microwave, despite many attempts. It might take a couple of tries to get the results you want.

Preparation for pressing is pretty quick; remove as much of the stems and foliage as desired, and make certain that the petals are lying flat and open, with no creases or folds, before you begin. Be sure that the flowers aren't touching one another. Of course, the fresh material should be dry before you start.

Traditional Book Pressing

Tried and true, nothing could be much easier than this ancient method. It's a very easy, very satisfying method of preserving flowers, perfect to use when you're strolling around your yard and find just one little beauty you want to save. Place your specimens between sheets of porous paper and close them inside a heavy book, wait a few weeks, and *voilà*—pressed flowers. Wax paper will also produce pretty decent results, and some sources suggest using newspaper, though I'm not enamored with that material. If the ink transfers to your flowers, they'll be ruined.

Using a Flower Press

Another perfectly easy technique is the use of the flower press. These devices are generally made with two pieces of wood, with layers of blotting paper and cardboard in between. Closures can vary, from screws and wing nuts to hook-and-loop tape, but the idea is the same, which is to keep the material pressed tightly between the wooden cover pieces during the drying cycle. Pressing times of several weeks will vary according to the flowers, but you should check them for progress. If the material is damp or soft, leave it for a bit longer.

Using a Microwave Flower Press

You can obtain astonishing results with a microwave flower press, in only about two minutes or so. If you want to make a quick personalized card, or adorn a gift like the bags on page 30, this method will give you exquisite material with which to work.

I use a terra-cotta press, though the first generation of microwave presses was made of wood. The newer ceramic presses are generally sold with absorbent wool felt layers and thin sheets of tightly woven fabric. The flowers are placed between the layers of fabric, which are sandwiched between the felt and the press, as in the photo on page 13. Then, place the press in the microwave for about two minutes or so, but here's the important part—cook in 30-second intervals, to avoid burning the flowers. Let the flowers cool between the layers of fabric before you remove them; if you don't, they'll likely begin to curl.

Preparation for this technique varies little from the other pressing methods. However, some flower varieties press more successfully when the individual petals are dried. This is true for varieties that have a thick calyx like marigolds, or a bell-shaped structure, like the lisianthus. Gently remove the petals first, and place them in the press individually. Arrange them so they lie flat and don't touch one another, as in the photo below.

Of course, not all flowers are suited to this method. Some colors just won't remain true with the microwave technique; my lovely deep rose pansies with delicate yellow centers faded to a rather depressing brown when pressed in the microwave. But the vibrancy of the lisianthus and the delicate, translucent quality of the poppies I've obtained with this method far overshadow the disappointments.

Be sure to keep a record of your pressing times, and include any other factors that may influence the outcome. If it usually takes two minutes to dry a pansy, you might discover that it takes a little bit longer if you've had a few rainy days, for instance. Jot down any information that may help you in future efforts.

SEALING DRIED AND PRESSED FLOWERS

Most preserved materials need to be sealed in some fashion to prevent them from reabsorbing moisture. This can happen rather quickly and drastically; don't remove items from silica gel and then leave them sitting out overnight. You'll probably wake to discover melted lilies in the place of your picture-perfect specimens. So, be sure to factor in this important part of the preservation process.

There are many products for this purpose. Some are preservatives, which can be used before and after crafting or arranging. Other products are designed only for use

Some blossoms can't be pressed whole, but you can remove the petals and press them separately.

This peony was dried in silica gel and then sprayed with three coats of surface sealant.

on specific types of flowers. Surface sealants work very nicely on silica-dried flowers. Acrylic sprays can be used as a final coat, if desired. Visit your local craft store and investigate the different products, because you may need one specific to your flower as well as your intended use. However, many of the sealants contain toxic ingredients, and should only be used with proper ventilation and protective gloves, if necessary.

Pressed flowers can be sealed prior to use. The edges of the flowers may want to curl, so sometimes this can be a bit frustrating. But it does produce a well-preserved blossom.

Depending upon your use, though, it may not be necessary to seal the flowers first; decoupage does a fine job of sealing most flowers in the course of the project.

A couple of notes about sealing: The level of humidity in the atmosphere has a big effect on the success of the sealing process. In general, try to seal only on sunny, calm days. If I have to remove some flowers from gel on a rainy day, I set them in foam, place them in a sealed container with a thin layer of gel on the bottom, and wait until the condi-

tions are more favorable. You don't want to seal moisture into the flowers; you want to seal it out.

Finally, though some sources recommend holding dried flowers and applying the sealant, I prefer to use the wire handles on the flowers and sink them into floral foam. Then, place them on a work surface to be sprayed.

STORING PRESERVED MATERIALS

Make sure that your flowers are absolutely dry before you consider storing them. Air-dried materials can be wrapped in paper and stored in boxes; you may want to toss in a few mothballs for insurance. Silica-dried materials should be stored in an airtight container, in a dry location away from sunlight; leave some silica crystals in the box for additional protection. Pressed flowers can be stored in a variety of ways, in envelopes or plastic sandwich bags, but be sure they remain flat to preserve their beauty. A sturdy box is good protection, too. You might want to consider labeling your storage containers, so you can quickly locate the items when you are ready to craft.

This trellis is a lovely way to display dried flowers and herbs. For project instructions, see page 33.

FLORAL TOOLS AND SUPPLIES

Okay, whether from your own garden or the craft store, you have dried flowers on hand and a project in mind. What else do you need? Probably not much more than you already have.

If you need to purchase any of these items, they are certainly on the inexpensive side and are readily available at craft stores or garden centers. Floral wire is helpful to secure flowers, as is floral tape. (Both of these materials are found in various colors, including green and brown.) To use floral tape properly, apply it with tension, because that allows the waxed tape to adhere to itself as you wrap. Floral foam is the basis for several projects in the book, and it's always handy to have on hand if you plan to dry your own flowers. It works wonderfully as a foundation for the dried flowers while you are sealing or removing silica gel, for instance. I usually store dried flowers mounted in foam blocks.

Floral pins are used to secure natural materials to a base. Sealants, floral preservatives, and acrylic sprays, discussed on pages 14 and 15, are important supplies. A good pair of garden snips or floral shears will probably come in handy, and a pair of pruners will be helpful if you are working with material with thick stems or twigs, like the kitchen trellis on page 33. You'll need a pair of wire cutters, too.

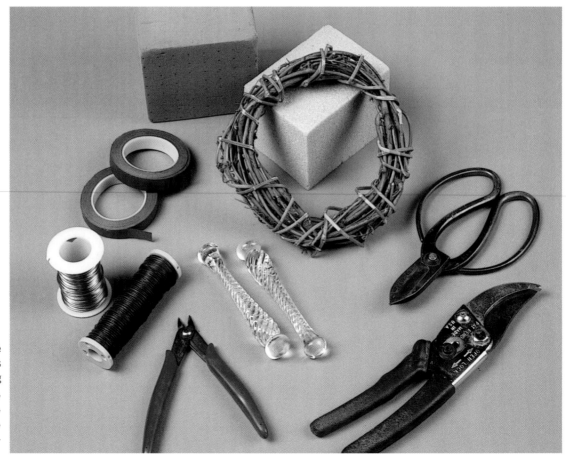

Here are some of the floral tools and supplies you will use, including foam, wreath forms, garden shears, pruners, pestles, wire cutters, wire, and floral tape.

CRAFTING TOOLS AND SUPPLIES

Most of the things that you need are very basic crafting supplies and need little explanation. A hot glue gun and glue sticks, decoupage medium, clear-drying craft glue, miscellaneous brushes, and scissors are essential to many of the projects. Basic sewing equipment, including a sewing machine, needles and thread, are used in the sachet bag on page 46, as well as several other projects. Beads, beading needles, and beading thread are used in

a few of the projects, and ribbons embellish several of them. Paper, both utilitarian and decorative, is an important ingredient in many of the projects. You'll need some sort of measuring device, a tape measure or ruler, and a pencil, pen, or marker. Most likely, you'll want to protect your work surface, perhaps with newspaper, craft paper, or waxed paper.

There are some specialized tools used in the book, like the eyelet punch used for the boxes on page 49. This project might give you a chance to work with some new equipment.

Of course, each set of instructions will detail the tools and supplies that you'll need to create that project.

Incorporate a new technique like simple embossing into your dried flower crafting.

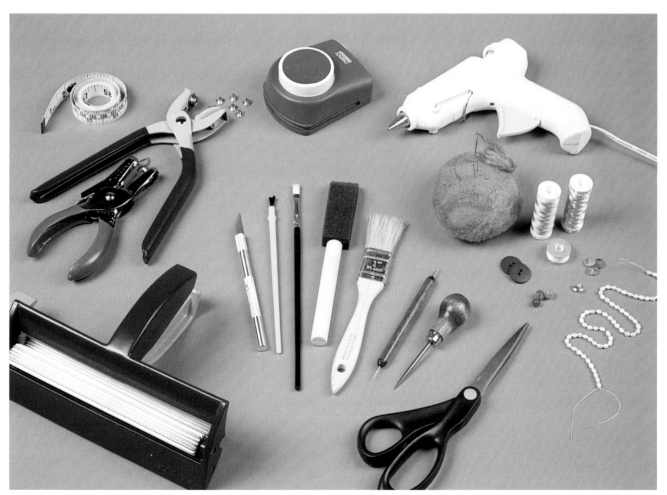

Pictured are many of the general crafting tools and supplies you will use to create the projects in this book. You probably already have most of them, including a glue gun, tape measure, sewing needles, beads, buttons, scissors, and paintbrushes.

CRAFTING TECHNIQUES, TIPS, AND CONSIDERATIONS

You can use dried or pressed flowers to embellish a craft project, like the perky little blossoms in the collection on page 42. Or, you might add dried materials as an ingredient in a project, like the soap and body products in the guest baskets on page 58. You can also use dried flowers as the basis for a project, as with the table runner on page 61. The techniques you use in each project will probably be very familiar to you, but the preserved material itself may have special characteristics that you need to keep in mind while you work. Here is some advice:

Embellishing a Project with Flowers

Generally speaking, use only clear-drying craft glue or decoupage medium if your project calls for a finishing coat of adhesive on top of the flowers. Other kinds of glue may leave you with a dull, clouded flower, not the vibrant specimen that you want. But even these two types have their differences. While I was experimenting with the curtain on page 63, I found that I could use craft glue successfully on the pink pansies, for instance, with no negative effects. But when used on the yellow varieties, the glue dried quite unattractively on the surface, and I switched to decoupage medium. It

To apply glue or decoupage medium to the back of a pressed petal, make the brush strokes from the inside to the outer edge of the petal (or from the center of the flower outward, as the case may be).

bears repeating that you should experiment with just a few specimens, using all the techniques you have in mind, before you begin a final project. It may save you some heartache.

When you are applying clear glue or decoupage medium on individual petals and don't plan to apply a top coat, try to use just the amount needed to coat the petal and no more. You may find that any excess will be impossible to remove from your base material, and it might spoil the appearance of your project. Use these supplies as sparingly as possible.

A flat paintbrush seems to work well when applying adhesives to the surfaces of pressed flowers. Work toward the outer edges of the flowers or petals, as shown in the photo above, making sure you don't paint decoupage over the blooms and onto your work surface—or you will have glued the flower to your table! The delicate nature of pressed flowers makes it difficult to remove them in these cases. I've lost many a nice blossom with a careless appli-

cation of glue. Be attentive as you work.

Your paintbrush is also an excellent tool for placing flowers on your project. Use just a bit of adhesive on the back of the flower, and then move it into place with the paintbrush, as shown in the photo below. While tweezers can also be used to transfer pressed flowers, the paintbrush method is virtually trouble-free and very easy, too.

Use a small paintbrush dipped in glue or decoupage medium to place the pressed flowers; dab the brush onto the back of the flower and move it into position.

Using Flowers as an Ingredient

Some interesting and unexpected things can happen to dried flowers when they are used in the crafting process. For instance, the purple disappears from pansies when they are placed into a soap medium. Oftentimes, commercially prepared dried flowers are dyed, and this color will then leach out when types of liquid ingredients are used. But the pansies that lost their color were pressed right from my garden, so dye was not the culprit. It's simply the nature of the plant itself. However, be advised that most store-bought materials will have been dyed and sealed, and these products may react with the ones you intend to use. A little test is probably in order before you begin.

This same phenomenon occurs with some types of sealants, too, such as water-based liquid products. These may cause certain colors to run, but they can also produce a rather intriguing antiqued look over the rest of the surface. You might find this to be a desirable quality in your final project, so experiment at will.

Making Flowers the Basis of a Project

Several of the projects that have the flowers themselves as the basic material also require floral foam. Though it is relatively easy to sink the stems into the foam, it may be helpful to make holes for the stems first; that way, you don't have to be overly concerned about possibly breaking a stem while you work. A variation of this technique is also used in the shadow box on page 39; it's demonstrated in the photo at right.

Of course, dried flowers are not as pliable as fresh flowers, and they won't have the graceful drape of a freshly cut blossom. But, there are a few tricks that you can employ to make working with these items easier. Floral preservatives, discussed on page 14, are often used by professionals before and after they begin

If you're certain that the flowers you're incorporating into a project have been dyed, like these neon pink beauties, you may want to test them first to make sure that they are color-fast.

to work; the preservatives soften the dried materials, which makes it easier to manipulate them while you are creating an arrangement. If you are using purchased materials and want to reshape the stems a bit, you can steam them just slightly and hold them in position as they dry. (You can rejuvenate a crushed bloom with this method, too.)

Because air-dried materials tend to have very straight stalks, you may wish to add some gentle curves with the following method. While the flowers are still fresh, insert a wire near the top of the stem for about an inch (2.5 cm). Then, gently wrap the wire around the length of the stem. After the flower has wilted just a bit, bend the wire to create some curves, and then allow it to dry fully.

When making an arrangement, particularly one like the stook on page 56, remove all the materials from their packaging and arrange the items so you can easily pick them up. Though this seems like a

Pierce holes into floral foam or foam core board with an awl and then place the flowers, as shown.

When you're dividing long material into shorter working pieces, be sure to break the stem at the proper point to prevent having any visible stems in your arrangement.

very simple idea, it really makes your work much easier if everything is readily accessible. Further, try to determine the desired height of the material that you're using and trim the stems first, if necessary.

To divide long material into shorter lengths, as you'll do for the wreaths on page 68, be sure to break the stem at the proper point, because you don't want any visible stems in your project. The stem should be snapped just at the location of the right thumb, as shown in the photo above. Then, you'll have a stem at the bottom of the left piece, and no visible stem at the top of the right piece. Repeat for as many pieces as needed, and glue the stem ends into place.

In most instances, arrangements using dried flowers are best worked from the center out, to prevent possible damage to the stems; with this method, you're not working over the material you've just placed. This may be contrary to the methods you use for fresh flowers, but try to plan your arrangements with this technique in mind, particularly if you're incorporating tall material.

Working Tips

Here's a no-brainer: Make sure that your material has been properly stored and kept fresh. If you add stale ingredients to a project such as the coasters on page 51, they won't release the lovely lavender scent as intended. This advice applies to all the projects, because they will certainly have more impact if the flowers you use are colorful and vivid, not faded and dusty.

Dried and pressed flowers are delicate. I've found that it's helpful to have a bit more material on hand than I really need, to account for breakage, bungled glue jobs, or other unintended mishaps.

Keep an eye on the ventilation in your workspace; pressed flowers can blow away with the slightest breeze, and you certainly don't want them to take flight into a container of decoupage medium! Consider the ambient humidity, too; if you are working with flowers that are not sealed, they could begin to absorb moisture quite rapidly.

Finally, each set of project instructions will give you some additional advice pertinent to that specific project, so look for some more tips in that section of the book.

DESIGN CONSIDERATIONS

Since you don't have to be concerned with containers that are waterproof when using dried flow-

Though dried flowers are delicate, they're not as fragile as you may think. They can be easily manipulated and arranged with just a bit of care.

ers, you can be very creative with the kinds of vessels you choose to use for arrangements. Basketry is an obvious example, but how about a bark container? Paper or cardboard boxes? Sections of bamboo? A pile of striking stones? Any kind of found object that can be used as a container is now at your disposal. The possibilities are endless.

Texture can create some visual interest in your projects; take a look at the burlap ribbon and corrugated cardboard on page 30 to see how these materials help highlight the delicate beauty of the pressed flowers.

Professional floral designers now say that the old rules about the ratio of the height of the container to the flowers can be tossed out the window. Now, it's far more important to size the arrangement in the context of its placement in your home, so consider where you plan to use the project. If it's on your dinner table, you want your guests to be able to converse and see each other clearly, so don't use a tall arrangement as a centerpiece.

Don't be overwhelmed by the quality of professionally produced arrangements you may have seen in floral shops or in people's homes. Some professional floral designers actually deconstruct flowers petal by petal, dry them in silica crystals, and then reconstruct them to use in arrangements, adding stems created from other materials. And many of those breathtaking dried floral displays have probably been treated with colored floral sprays to enhance the hues of the blooms. The professionals are, after all, professionals, so please remember that the goal of this book is to enjoy crafting with dried flowers. If you are new to this medium, allow some time to become acquainted with the nuances of working with preserved materials.

PURCHASING TIPS

Since dried materials can be expensive, make sure that you are purchasing top-quality flowers. Since they are generally sold in cellophane packages, inspect them to make sure

You don't need professional training to create a beautiful arrangement with dried flowers.

Purchased materials can be very lovely, and you may find some unusual items in stores, such as the Protea shown at the center bottom of the photo above.

that the flowers are mostly intact; if you see lots of loose material in the package, keep on looking. Likewise, since many of the store-bought materials have been dyed, make sure that the color hasn't faded.

Many florists also carry preserved materials. Though their prices are likely to be higher than at a craft store, their flowers may be locally grown, probably handled less, and perhaps in better condition. Lastly, try to determine the amount you need as best you can, to avoid unnecessary expense.

MAINTENANCE CONSIDERATIONS

Now that you have created a project with dried flowers, there are several things that you can do to increase its longevity. Obviously, through the course of time, the materials will age. But some sources say that dried flowers can be kept for years, if they are cared for properly.

First, keep your projects out of the bright sun, to reducing fading. Try to avoid placing dried materials in rooms that can be damp or humid, like a bathroom or kitchen. (A few projects in this book are delightful exceptions to this rule, however.) If your project becomes dusty, you can use a hair dryer on a low, cool setting to disperse the particles. Try a paintbrush, too, for just a quick touch-up.

Finally, for safety's sake, you should keep it away from sparks

To keep your dried flowers looking this lovely, seal them well; keep them in a dry place; and don't display them in direct sunlight.

and flames, as the materials are, of course, very dry. The sealant products are flammable as well.

GETTING STARTED

If you're interested in working with dried flowers, I think you'll find that this book will satisfy your curiosity. The information presented lets you get involved at a level that suits you and your lifestyle, either starting with your own materials or with purchased ones. You may find that you can appreciate the subtleties of flowers a little bit more when you work with them as closely as you will in these projects. Now, turn the page and begin!

Flower Fun

There are many simple ways you can use dried flowers in crafting or decorating, so fast and easy that they really don't need detailed instructions. Here are a few additional suggestions to incorporate preserved materials into your life:

ℚ Decoupage individual petals or whole pressed flowers onto paper and line your drawers. A bit more elegant than regular shelf paper, don't you think?

ℚ Similarly, take a few petals or small flowers and glue them inside an envelope; it adds a nice touch for a special piece of correspondence.

ℚ There are several different ways you can adorn gifts with dried or pressed flowers. When you are tying the ribbon into a bow, place a few stems of your favorite dried flowers in the knot. Sprinkle a handful of petals over a wrapped package for a stunning presentation, or attach a large dramatic flower like a peony with metallic wire, rather than ribbon.

ℚ For a twist on wrapping paper, use two layers of paper and place pressed flowers between the two; just make sure the material on top is transparent or translucent, so use cellophane or vellum, for example.

ℚ Armature wire, available from art and craft suppliers, can be used as a sleek, modern way to bind bunches of flowers into simple, stand-alone displays.

ℚ Create whimsical stems for dried flowers from wire. Use pliers to bend or wrap the wire into the design of your choice, remove most of the original stem, and use floral tape to attach the lengths of wire to the remaining stem. Don't worry about covering up the tape; this idea revolves around fun. Display in a clear container, or just sink into floral foam for a kitschy arrangement.

ℚ Fill a clear vase or bowl with flower heads instead of fruit; large showy species are perfect for this idea.

ℚ Try pressed flowers to create custom switch plates for your walls. At your local home improvement center, you can find clear plastic switch plates designed to be backed with wallpaper; instead, use a decorative paper and pressed flowers or foliage of your choice.

Drawer Pulls

DESIGNER: JOAN MORRIS

Aren't these wonderful? And so simple, too. The glass craft stones create the illusion that the flowers are embedded in the drawer pulls; they also produce a magnifying effect that brilliantly displays the blossoms. Retrofit any cabinet using this technique. The stones aren't perfectly circular, so expect these pulls to be delightfully imperfect.

YOU WILL NEED

Clear glass craft stones, 1¼ inches (3.1 cm) in diameter

Decoupage medium

Small paintbrushes

Statice, assorted colors

Pansies

White paint

Hot glue gun and glue sticks, or cyanoacrylate glue

Concave drawer pulls, 1⅜ inches (3.4 cm) in diameter— from a home improvement store

Screwdriver

VARIATION

The stones are available in pastel tones, too, and you may find these useful in coordinating a look for your home decorating. This method can be used to create ornamentation for curtain tiebacks (add a pin finding to the back of the stones), or make elegant magnets (add a magnet or adhesive magnetic strip to the back).

1 On the flat side of a glass stone, paint on the decoupage medium. Then, place alternating colors of statice on the lower part of the glass piece, arranging them in a half-circle. Paint on a little more decoupage medium. As shown, place the pansy face-down behind the statice layer, using individual petals if desired. Cover the rest of the glass piece. Paint a light layer of decoupage medium on the back of the pansy to flatten the petals. Let dry. Repeat for as many drawer pulls as needed.

3 Glue the flower-covered stones to the drawer pulls. Center the stones on the pulls and press in place. Be certain to use enough glue to securely fasten the stones, since the pulls may get a lot of use. Let dry.

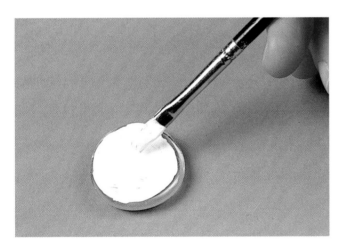

2 Paint over the back of the glass piece with white paint, completely covering the flowers. This application of paint makes the glass stones opaque and prevents the finish of the drawer pull from detracting from the design of the pressed flowers. Let the piece dry, and then repeat for the other drawer pulls.

4 Choose a location for the hardware, and then install the drawer pulls, using the screws that are sold with the hardware. Rotate the pulls as needed for the correct orientation of the design on the stones.

TIP: Glass craft stones and drawer pulls are available in different sizes, but the smaller sizes will be a bit more difficult to use for this project.

Translucent Lamp

DESIGNER: CORINNE KURZMANN

You may have admired a similar design in a trendy boutique, and now you can create your own using pressed flowers and translucent handmade paper. When you illuminate it, the flowers glow from within, displaying their intricate silhouettes. It's a lovely, subtle lighting treatment.

YOU WILL NEED

Lamp form—from a craft store

Light bulb

Ruler

Pencil

Translucent handmade paper (with petals, if desired)

Scissors or decorative-edged scissors

Pressed flowers

Decoupage medium

Paintbrush

Hole punch or nail

Small bookbinding screws

Vellum or squares of handmade paper (optional)

TIP: Remember that the paper you choose should be somewhat translucent. You may wish to experiment with different weights of paper before you begin, by wrapping them around the form when it's illuminated. That way, you can be sure that you'll obtain the desired results when your lampshade is finished.

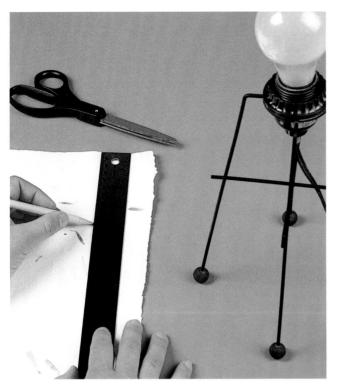

1 Measure, mark, and cut the paper to the desired size, based on your lamp form. Then, cut a second sheet the same size, as you will need two layers of paper for the shade. Use decorative-edged scissors to cut the paper, if desired, or tear along the edges to create the same effect.

2 Lay one of the sheets of paper flat on a work surface and arrange the dried flowers. Then, use the decoupage medium to glue the flowers in place, being careful to use a minimal amount of the decoupage so it doesn't bleed through the paper.

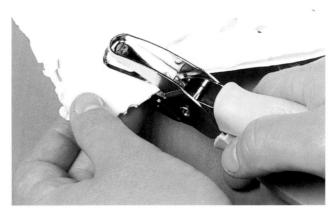

3 To align the holes for the shade, place one of the sheets of paper around the form and mark the locations of the holes that will fit on the frame. Next, place the paper back on your work surface and mark the spots to install the bookbinder's screws, spaced evenly along the edges of the paper. Then, align the two sheets and use the hole punch or nail to make the holes through both layers.

4 Put the two sheets together, with the pressed flower layer on the inside. Remove the caps on the lamp form, if necessary, to slip the paper onto the form; then replace the caps. Place the holes for the bookbinder's screws at the back post of the lamp form and insert the screws at the marked spots, as shown. Add layers of vellum underneath the screws or between the layers of paper if you feel that your lampshade needs the extra support.

Floral Spheres

DESIGNER: TERRY TAYLOR

Your guests won't stop talking about this clever arrangement featuring helichrysum, probably better known by its common name, strawflower. It is very easy to grow, so you can plan this project in the spring, cultivate it through the summer, and enjoy it in the fall. Or, go ahead and purchase dried strawflowers now, if you just can't wait to make this centerpiece.

YOU WILL NEED

Polystyrene foam balls, a variety of sizes

Pencil

Polystyrene foam square

Acrylic paint

Flat paintbrush

4 bunches of strawflowers

Hot glue gun and glue sticks

Small bowl or container

Vine-wrapped bamboo

Craft knife or small saw

Wire

Raffia

1 Use an old pencil to temporarily position one of the balls into the polystyrene foam. Paint the ball with a coat of acrylic paint that matches the color of your strawflowers, and let them dry completely. Don't skip this step, because it keeps the color of the ball from peeking through your glued plant material.

2 Remove the flower heads from the stems, leaving as little stem material as possible. Hot glue strawflowers to the top of the ball, as shown, placing the flowers as closely together as possible. After you have partially covered the ball, take it off its pencil stand and move it to a small container so you can rotate the ball as needed to finish gluing on the flowers. Repeat steps 1 and 2 to create the desired number of spheres.

3 Cut three equal lengths of bamboo to use for a tripod. Cross two sticks at an angle, as shown, and wrap them tightly with wire where they cross. Try to make this joint very secure, as this forms the base of the tripod.

4 Fiddle with the placement of the third leg of the tripod; this is art, not science! When you are satisfied with the way it looks and stands, use a bit of hot glue to hold the three sticks together. For extra security, wrap a length of wire around the tripod, as shown.

5 To cover the joint in the tripod, use raffia to disguise the wire and hot glue. You may need to use several lengths of raffia, using a bit of hot glue to secure the strands. Repeat steps 3, 4, and 5 to build as many tripods as needed.

VARIATIONS

Hot glue still-pliable autumn leaves to a ball, and then randomly wrap metallic thread around and around the ball to accent them. Cover the balls with dried seed-pods of lunaria (money plant) for a sleek, wintertime look. Use this same technique on a smaller scale to create holiday ornaments.

Blooming Gift Bags

DESIGNER: VALERIE SHRADER

Why use a bow when you can use a flower instead?
Here's a new way to adorn a gift without wrap or ribbon. Use dried petals
to create your own fanciful flowers, adding beads or metallic threads to enhance
your design. Collaborate with nature to make great cards, too.

YOU WILL NEED

Waxed paper

Dried lisianthus and Gerber daisies, individual petals

Decoupage medium

Flat paintbrush

Parchment paper—from a kitchen specialty shop

Heavy book

Scissors

Assorted beads

Beading needle

Beading thread

Corrugated gift bags, assorted sizes

Burlap ribbon

Silver metallic thread

Sewing needle

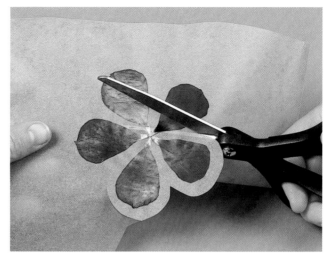

2 After the flower is dry, trim around the parchment paper to create the frame for the flower, as shown. Depending upon the type of beads you choose, either sew them carefully at the center of the flower or glue them in place with the decoupage medium. If you glued beads into the center, let the glue dry before you proceed to the next step.

1 To make the beaded flowers on the large bag, first cover your work surface with waxed paper. Create the flower shape on a piece of parchment paper by carefully painting decoupage medium on the back of the petals, as shown, and gluing them into place, one at a time. Try not to let the decoupage spread onto the parchment paper. Smooth the petals into place gently with your fingertips. Place a layer of waxed paper over the top, and then let your flower dry thoroughly inside a heavy book.

3 Before you attach the flowers, first decide on their placement on the bag. Then, paint decoupage medium onto the back of the center of the flower and press it onto the bag. Place the bag on its back while the decoupage is drying.

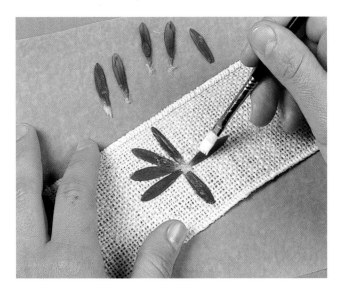

4 To create the flowers on the burlap ribbon, first cut the ribbon to the length of your bag. Then, place a small dab of decoupage medium on the back of the first petal and begin to build your flower at the desired location along the ribbon. Press into place, and add more petals as needed. Paint decoupage medium on the top of the petals also, working from the inside to the outer edge, to secure them in the design. Let dry, and then embellish the center with silver beads. Use the silver metallic thread to attach the ribbon to the bag, taking just a few stitches at the center of the ribbon at the top and bottom of the bag.

TIP: Experiment with other wide-petal flowers to create this look. Some species of poppy dry to a beautiful, translucent finish, for example.

You can have a lot of fun using complete flowers with this process, too, as you can see in the photo below. Use pressed daisies and decoupage them onto a piece of natural burlap; then make a pocket on the front of the bag by attaching the burlap with metallic thread. Or, dry osteospermum and glue them onto parchment paper, stitch the paper onto a piece of white burlap with decorative thread, and glue the entire piece onto the top of a corrugated box. Lastly, many dried flowers look beautiful when they are decoupaged onto mesh ribbon—they almost seem to melt into the fabric.

Kitchen Trellis

DESIGNER: SUSAN MCBRIDE

This beautiful arrangement of twigs, twine, and blossoms is decorative and functional, too, as you can use this trellis as a drying rack for herbs or flowers. Use found materials from your yard to create the twig framework, and embellish as desired with your favorites from the garden. Enlarge this design if you need more drying space.

YOU WILL NEED

Large-gauge sewing needle

Dark brown thread

Rubber gloves

Dried flowers and herbs—oregano, yarrow, chili peppers

Scissors

Hemp twine

9 thin hardwood twigs

2 thick hardwood twigs

Pruners or garden snips

TIP: Try to hang your trellis in a dry area in the kitchen, away from the humidity of boiling water.

VARIATION

Consider an Asian influence for this project, and use bamboo to create the trellis. Look for decorative twine if you want a more polished look.

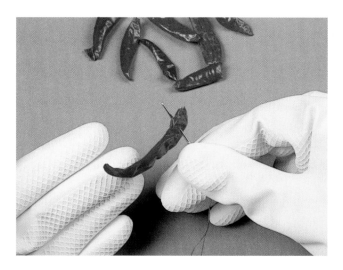

1 Using the needle and the brown thread, carefully pierce the chili peppers and thread them onto a length of thread about 7 inches (17.8 cm) long. (Since the chili peppers contain capsicum that burns the skin, you should wear rubber gloves. If you don't, you'd better not rub your eyes while you're working on this portion of the project!) Once you have about a dozen peppers on the thread, tie them together in a circle.

3 Find twigs with about the same diameter, and use the pruners or garden snips to cut nine twigs to a length of about 12 inches (30.5 cm); these twigs will form the horizontal supports for the trellis. Find two thicker twigs and cut these to a length of about 18 inches (45.7 cm); these are the vertical supports. Take the thinner twigs and bind the edges into three bundles of three twigs each, as shown. Attach these bundles to the longer, thicker twigs by tying on with hemp twine. Since this is a rustic design, the binding doesn't have to be exact, but do trim the edges to keep it neat.

2 Cut the stems of the oregano to about 4½ inches (11.4 cm). Bind three to five stems together with a length of hemp twine about 18 inches (45.7 cm) long. Make three small bouquets, and then use the same technique to make two small yarrow bouquets; be certain to leave enough twine to tie the bouquets onto the twig trellis. Set aside.

4 Attach the herb bouquets and the bunches of peppers to the twig trellis as desired. Take a length of the hemp twine and create a loop for hanging, being sure that you tie the knots securely so the trellis doesn't fall.

Decorated Lampshade

DESIGNER: TERRY TAYLOR

A length of ribbon and a few dried flowers will dress up any lampshade. This is a quick and easy project, easily adapted to your decor, and a good one for a beginner to get the feel of working with dried materials. Have a little fun with this decorating idea; it's the perfect excuse to experiment with color and texture.

YOU WILL NEED

Lampshade

Tape measure

Ribbon

Scissors

Sewing needle

Thread

Hot glue gun and glue sticks

Dried flowers

VARIATION

Create some simple holiday looks for your home with this technique. It's an easy and inexpensive way to add seasonal color; attach small pinecones or berries, perhaps, or small glass ornaments to accent the dried flowers you choose.

1 Determine the circumference of your lamp-shade, and then cut a length of ribbon two to three times that measurement. The longer the ribbon length, the fuller the ruffle you'll create. Consider the type of flowers you will use as you decide how full to make the ruffle.

2 Thread your needle with a double strand of thread, in a color complementary to your ribbon. Knot the end. Sew a line of ¼-inch (6 mm) basting stitches down the center of the ribbon, but leave the thread in the needle.

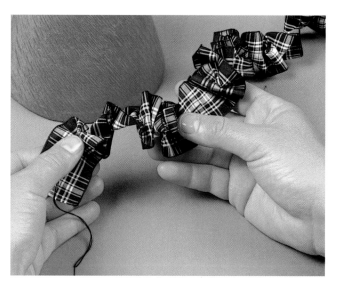

3 Gather the ribbon on the thread by pulling the basting stitches. Use your fingers to evenly distribute the gathers as desired. When you are satisfied with the appearance of the ribbon, knot the thread.

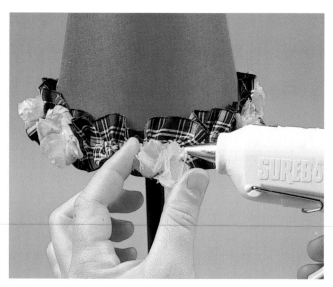

4 Hot glue the ribbon to the base of the shade, letting the ribbon extend approximately ½ inch (1.3 cm) below the base of the shade. Then, hot glue flowers to the ribbon; place them by sight or measure to assure that the flowers are evenly distributed along the ruffled border.

Tonal Arrangement

DESIGNER: VALERIE SHRADER

Take a minimalist approach when you create this arrangement of larkspur, using only similar shades of blue. Start with a distinctive organic container, and then plan your arrangement with only one type of flower for a lush, contemporary look. The effect is simple, yet dramatic.

Rusted container

Block of floral foam

Kitchen knife

4 bunches of larkspur, 2 light blue and 2 dark blue

Garden snips or pruners (optional)

Floral preservative (optional)

2 Snap the stems of the larkspur to the desired length; use the snips for this step if your flowers have thick stalks. Then, begin to build the arrangement in the middle of the foam, starting with the longest stalks of larkspur. Angle the ends of the stems toward the center to create a spray of blossoms. Continue to add the light blue larkspur until you've used about two-thirds of the first bunch, slightly decreasing the height as you work.

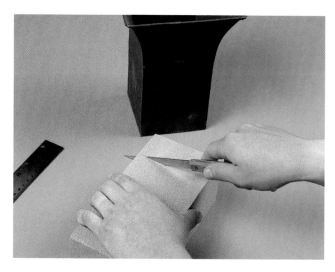

1 Fit the foam into the container. Use the kitchen knife to carve the foam into the proper shape to ensure a snug fit. Leave 1 or 2 inches (2.5 or 5 cm) of space between the top of the foam and the top of the container; this will allow you some working room to create the arrangement.

3 Now, begin to intersperse a few stalks of the dark blue larkspur, gradually using less light blue larkspur and more dark blue stems. Continue to angle them toward the center and decrease the height of the larkspur, creating a full, luxurious arrangement. When you are content with your project, spray it with floral preservative, if desired.

TIP: Your dried flower arrangements will last longer if they are not displayed in the bright sunlight, so keep this idea in mind when you use this project to decorate your home.

VARIATION

In the right container, you can use a dense arrangement of stems that are all the same height to create a carpet of flowers.

Compass Shadow Box

DESIGNER: JOAN MORRIS

Does this design look familiar? It's based on a quilting pattern, and it offers infinite possibilities for variations in color and texture. Use all pressed flowers, for instance; for a more rustic feel, add some twigs or acorns. You'll find that it's simple to disassemble the shadow box to craft this project.

YOU WILL NEED

Foam core board, ½ inch (1.3 cm) thick

Ruler

Pencil

Utility knife

Shadow box, 8 x 8 inches (20.3 x 20.3 cm)

White paper (optional)

Scissors

Transfer paper

Assorted dried flowers

Hot glue gun and glue sticks

Awl

1 Measure and mark the foam board to create a piece that is 7¾ x 7¾ inches (19.7 x 19.7 cm). Using the utility knife, cut the piece to these dimensions, as shown; after you've cut this piece, make sure it fits tightly inside the shadow box. Next, measure, mark, and cut the piece of paper to 7¾ x 7¾ inches (19.7 x 19.7 cm).

2 Trace or draw your chosen design onto the white paper. (To replicate this design, use the template on page 78.) Then, take the transfer paper and trace the design onto the foam core board; however, if you're confident in your drawing skills, simply transfer the design directly to the foam core board.

3 Decide which flowers to use in each element of the design, balancing the color and shape of the materials. Remove the flowers from their stalks; if possible, leave a short stem at the base of the flower to insert into the board. Start from the center of the design and use the glue gun to place the flowers; use the awl to make a hole for the materials with stems, place the flowers into the holes, and then glue into place. Flat materials, like eucalyptus, can be glued directly onto the board.

4 When you've completed the design, carefully place the frame over the foam core board, inserting it into the box. Hang or display as desired.

TIP: Since quilting books inspired the design in this project, you might look to these sources for other ideas.

VARIATION

The shadow box in this project was painted to complement the colors of its dried flowers. You may choose to retain the natural finish of your box, if it enhances your design; you could also make a box from salvaged materials, if you're handy with tools.

More Flower Fun

Ⓒ Create your own botanical pictures with pressed flowers and foliage. Find a frame you like, and then add the dried materials. Use a layer of linen or decorative paper underneath the flowers for contrast, if desired.

Ⓒ Find some salvaged materials and use them to display dried flowers. Look for some pieces of old ceiling tin and glue on some miniature roses; put two or three together for a grouping. Likewise, you might discover some old barn planks filled with fortuitous cracks; cut the planks into short pieces and insert some stems into the planks, and then hang for a rustic display.

Flower Power Collection

DESIGNERS: ALLISON SMITH & TERRY TAYLOR

Sock it to me! These projects have in common the use of some fun little pressed flowers in funky neon colors, reminiscent of the '60s. Add decoupage and a dash of imagination to create this groovy grouping of items.

YOU WILL NEED

(FOR THE VOTIVES)

Craft glue

Water

Small container

Small soft paintbrush

Lime green votive candles

Small pink pressed flowers

Paraffin

Double boiler

Plastic container

Wax paper

(FOR THE PILLARS)

Tape measure

Tall glass emergency candle

Orange high fiber content handmade paper

Scissors

Decoupage medium

Foam paintbrush

Small orange pressed flowers, coordinated to the paper color

(FOR THE FRAMES)

Patterned tissue paper

Scissors

Paper frame

Decoupage medium

Small container

Small paintbrush

Small pink pressed flowers

Craft glue

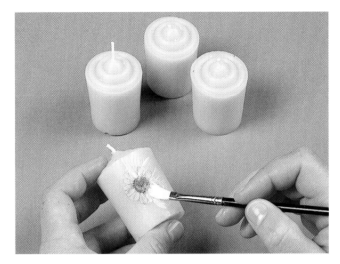

1 To craft the votives, begin by diluting the glue with water by one half. With the paintbrush, apply a small amount of glue onto the candle where the flower is to be placed. Press the flower onto the candle and gently paint over the candle to seal it, as shown. Be careful not to make bubbles in the glue by overworking it. Let the votive dry completely before the next step.

2 Use an old plastic container to melt the paraffin in a double boiler. Once you use a container to melt wax, it can't be used for any other purpose; on the other hand, the paraffin can be used again and again for other projects. When the paraffin is completely melted, hold the candle by the wick and quickly dip it only *one time* into the paraffin. Make one swift motion as you dip and remove. Don't allow the candle to sit in the paraffin bath or it will cloud

the colors of the candle and flower. Repeat steps 1 and 2 for as many votives as desired; then, let them dry on wax paper.

affixing each with a small dot of decoupage medium. Lastly, seal by painting over the entire candle with decoupage medium.

3 To decorate the pillar candle, first measure the candle and cut the paper to the dimensions of the candle, adding 1 inch (2.5 cm) to the height and ½ inch (1.3 cm) to the circumference of the candle. Cover the candle with decoupage medium; if the medium is too thick, thin it down with water. Place the paper on a flat surface, and then put the candle on top of the paper and roll the candle so the paper adheres to it, as shown. Smooth it with your hands.

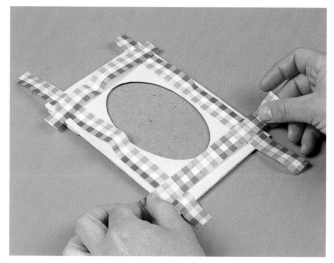

5 For the decorated frame, cut the tissue paper into strips proportionate to your frame. Arrange the strips as you would like to see them on the frame, as shown; you might try several arrangements until you find one that you like. Cut the strips slightly longer than the frame's dimensions; you will eventually fold the strips to the back of the frame. For now, set the strips to the side.

4 Turn the candle upside down and spread decoupage medium onto the bottom of the candle. Press the paper down and allow it to dry. Add the flowers randomly over the candle, as shown,

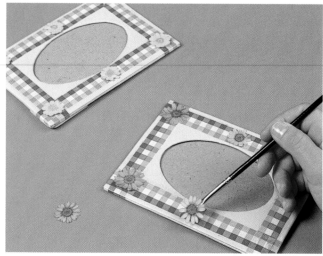

6 To decorate the frame, pour a small amount of decoupage medium into the container. Brush a coat of the medium onto the frame the width of one of your strips. Lay one of the strips of tissue onto the

medium, and use your fingers or the brush to smooth the tissue into place. Adhere all of the strips in this manner. Then, brush the medium onto the back of the frame, and fold over all of the tissue ends. Smooth them into place. Allow the strips to dry and then use white craft glue to adhere pressed flowers to the face of the frame, as shown.

TIP: Be sure you leave enough space to insert the photo after you've enhanced the picture frame.

VARIATIONS

Press colorful autumn leaves and use them instead of flowers in any of these projects. Rather than a paper frame, use a wooden frame; simply paint the frame before you apply the tissue and dried floral embellishments.

Ribbon Sachet Bag

DESIGNER: JOAN MORRIS

This delicate creation is the perfect complement to a fragrant blend of potpourri. If you want to make your own potpourri, choose your favorite materials and assemble the mixture, then exercise a little patience, as it will take about six weeks to cure. In the meantime, find some glorious ribbons to make this bag and dream about the scented result.

YOU WILL NEED

(FOR THE BAG)

½ yard (.45 m) of burgundy mesh ribbon,
2 inches (5 cm) wide

½ yard (.45 m) of off-white mesh wired ribbon,
5 inches (12.7 cm) wide

Sewing needle

Invisible thread

Scissors

Hem gauge

Sewing machine

Thread

1 yard (.9 m) of burgundy satin ribbon, ¼ inch (6 mm) wide

Rubber band

(FOR THE POTPOURRI)

Fragrant dried materials

Bowl

Fixative

Essential oil (optional)

Paper bag

2 Find the center of the ribbon by folding it in half lengthwise, wrong sides together, so that the narrow ribbon is on the outside. Machine stitch the sides together close to the edges to form the bag. Make sure the wired edges don't get caught in the seam.

1 To make the bag, begin by placing the 2-inch-wide (5 cm) ribbon in the center of the 5-inch-wide (12.7 cm) ribbon. Hand stitch the narrow ribbon onto the wider ribbon along its length, using invisible thread. (A sewing machine may also be used for this step, if desired.) Turn under a ½-inch (1.3 cm) hem on both raw edges and stitch in place.

3 To make a potpourri, choose fragrant dried materials and place them into a bowl; add 1 tablespoon (15 ml) of fixative for each cup of potpourri. (The potpourri for this project was chosen to coordinate with the color of the ribbon.) If desired, add just a few drops of essential oil for extra fragrance. Mix thoroughly and place in the paper bag; shake well and then roll the bag tightly to remove excess air. Store in a dark location and shake once a day for a week; then shake once a week for the next five weeks.

If you plan on placing your sachet bag deep within a drawer, you can omit the floral decoration in step 4 so it will lie flat.

4 To decorate your bag, glue three or four eucalyptus leaves together to form a base. Then, add a layer of dried material, next a circle of statice, and finally a single dried flower in the center, gluing each layer on successively. Lastly, glue the arrangements onto the center of the ribbon.

5 When the potpourri is ready, fill the ribbon bag within 2½ inches (6.4 cm) of the top. Then, gather the bag about 2 inches (5 cm) from the top, and secure with a rubber band. Wrap the ¼-inch-wide (6 mm) ribbon around the rubber band and make a bow. Of course, if you don't want to make your own potpourri, you can purchase it ready-made and add it to the bag.

Rose and Moss Boxes

DESIGNER: TERRY TAYLOR

This is a versatile project with as many variations as there are colors of paint and types of dried flowers. The plain boxes are like blank canvases, ready to be transformed to suit your mood and tastes. Use these embellished boxes to store treasured mementos, or to store nothing at all, for that matter—they don't have to be functional to be appreciated.

YOU WILL NEED

Paper boxes

Off-white acrylic paint

Paintbrushes

Masking tape

Metallic acrylic paint

Paper towels

Tape measure

Pencil

Hole punch

Eyelet punch and eyelets

Dried miniature rosebuds

Scissors

Reindeer moss (or similar dried moss)

Hot glue gun and glue sticks

1 yard (.9 m) of ribbon

VARIATIONS

Use bright paint colors and tiny strawflowers for a summery look. Or, for an autumnal accent, glue tiny acorns around the box lid. Dried poppy seed heads and a dash of wintry white glitter sprinkled all over the box would make an unusually festive holiday decoration.

1 Paint the lid and box with one coat of acrylic paint. Let them dry thoroughly, and then apply a second coat of paint. Let the box dry completely.

2 Place a length of masking tape above and below the embossed band around the box. Paint the band with metallic paint, then quickly wipe off the paint, as shown. Remove the tape when dry.

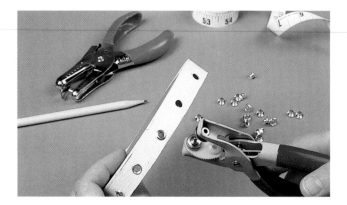

3 Measure and make an even number of marks around the rim of the box lid, spacing them at regular intervals. Use the hole punch to pierce a hole at each mark. Then, use the eyelet punch to set an eyelet in each hole, as shown.

4 Trim the stem from the bottom of each minia-ture rosebud. Hot glue a single row of closely spaced rosebuds around the edge of the box lid. Then, fill in the center of the box lid with reindeer moss, attaching it with hot glue, as shown.

5 Cut the ribbon to the desired length. Then, thread the ribbon through the eyelets. Wrap the ends of the ribbon with masking tape, if desired, to make it easier to thread. Lastly, tie a bow with the ribbon ends.

Aromatic Coasters

DESIGNER: ALLISON SMITH

These sweet little coasters are filled with a surprise—lavender, which releases its fragrance each time you set your hot mug atop them. Make a set of four to safeguard your furniture, and you'll be protecting your sanity at the same time with the soothing aroma of lavender, known for its relaxing properties. Choose an antiqued fabric for this mood-lifting project.

YOU WILL NEED
(FOR FOUR COASTERS)

Paper

Compass

Scissors

Pins

¼ yard (22.9 cm) of floral print fabric

Sewing machine

Thread

Wooden spoon

Iron and ironing board

Lavender flowers

Spoon

4 decorative buttons, each 1 inch (2.5 cm) in diameter

Sewing needle

Embroidery floss

1 Use the compass to make a paper pattern that is 5¼ inches (13.3 cm) in diameter; cut it out with the scissors. Then, pin to the fabric and cut out the circles; to make four coasters, you'll need eight circles.

2 Place two of the circles with their right sides together. Then, sew them together using a ⅝-inch (1.6 cm) seam allowance. Leave a 2-inch (5 cm) gap in the seam, so you have an opening to fill the coasters with lavender.

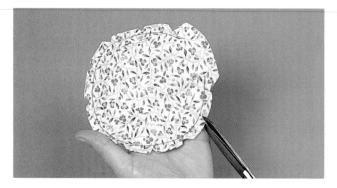

3 Trim the seams along the inside edges. Then, snip along the inside edge close to the seam line, as shown, but avoid cutting the seam. Turn the coaster right side out and push out the edges with the end of a wooden spoon. Press flat.

4 Fill the coasters with lavender to a depth of roughly ¼ inch (6 mm), and distribute the lavender evenly inside the coaster. (Lavender is available in bulk, with the flowers already removed from the stalks. This form of lavender is ideal to use in this project.) Hand stitch the opening closed.

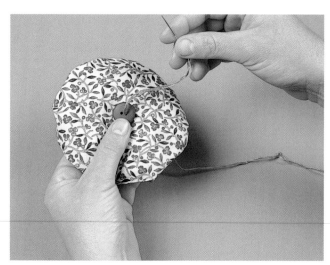

5 Sew the button onto the center of the coaster using the embroidery floss; choose a color of floss and button that complements your fabric. Tie a decorative knot on top and trim the ends. Repeat steps 2 though 5 to make the other three coasters.

VARIATIONS

Experiment with sachet or fine potpourri to fill these coasters, too; a translucent fabric would provide an elegant touch.

Wrapped Mirror

DESIGNER: TERRY TAYLOR

The elegant and exotic pitcher plant is showcased on this decorative accent mirror. The intricate wrapping of the raffia creates the perfect textured backdrop for the dried pitchers. Don't even think about making this project for a gift; you need to keep this mirror for yourself.

2 Wrap the raffia around the width of the top and bottom of the frame. Hot glue the ends of the raffia to the back of the frame as you work. Don't skimp on the raffia! Too much is better than too little; otherwise, you'll have foam peeking out unexpectedly (and probably unpleasantly, too).

1 Measure and mark a 5 x 7-inch (12.7 x 17.8 cm) rectangle in the center of the foam form. Use the serrated kitchen knife to saw out the rectangle. Save the rectangle and recycle it into some other craft project.

3 Now, wrap the raffia around the length of the sides of the frame, from top to bottom. Again, be generous with the raffia, and use an amount consistent with that on the top and bottom of the frame. Hot glue to the frame as you work, as in step 2.

4 Wrap the middle sections of the sides, top, and bottom of the frame with raffia, as shown, so that all of the foam is covered. As in the previous steps, hot glue the ends to the back of the frame.

5 Use the hot glue gun and affix the mirror to the back of the frame. Then, glue the pitcher plants to the frame. If desired, accent the plant material with a decorative button or bead, as shown, and add the mirror hanger.

ADVISORY

Be certain to use only cultivated pitcher plants (members of the genus *Sarracenia*) in this or any other project, as most varieties are endangered in the wild.

VARIATIONS

Wrap several stems of dried wheat with raffia in place of the pitcher plants. Or, hot glue trimmed bamboo stalks to the edges of the wrapped frame.

More Flower Fun

☙ Add some romance to a strand of paper lanterns by decoupaging dried flowers or petals onto the globes.

☙ You can preserve edible flowers by sugaring or crystallizing them; paint the petals or flowers with a wash of egg white, then use a strainer to sprinkle on the sugar. Leave them to dry in a warm location, and use them within three days as decorations for desserts. One of the loveliest cakes I've ever seen was decorated with sugared native violets.

☙ For a simple but elegant display, place a row of single dried roses along the wall. It's the perfect decorating touch for a guest room.

New Age Stook

DESIGNERS: VALERIE SHRADER & TERRY TAYLOR

Here is the evolution of the stook—the shocks of corn or wheat that farmers left to dry in the field. The wheat in this arrangement keeps it true to its origins, but the addition of the Protea sends this stook straight to the twenty-first century. This is also the same basic technique used to create posies, smaller arrangements usually made with fresh flowers.

YOU WILL NEED

6 stalks of Protea
3 packages of wheat
Floral tape or twine
Wire
Wire cutters
Mesh ribbon, wide and narrow
Scissors
Decorative paper

1 Place all the materials within reach, and spread them out so they are easy to grab; once you begin to assemble the stook, it's difficult to put it down without compromising its shape. Arrange the tape or twine so you're working with the loose end of the spool or roll, but keep it in one continuous strand.

2 Take three or four pieces of wheat to begin the stook and wrap tightly with the tape just under the heads of the wheat. Continue to add three or four stems at a time until you're happy with the size of the crown, wrapping at the same spot just under the heads after each addition.

4 Wrap around the tape with wire; this stabilizes the stook so you can add the decorative elements. Next, cover the wire with a layer of mesh ribbon; then a layer of decorative paper; and finally a layer of narrow mesh ribbon. Use the hot glue gun to secure each layer as you add it, gluing each addition to the layer underneath it if necessary.

3 Now, you will begin to decrease the height of the material in the stook. Take a handful of stems and add at an angle, continuing to wrap tightly after each addition and still leaving tape connected to the roll. Add stems around all sides of the stook until you are satisfied with the shape, adding the Protea as desired.

5 To make the stook stand upright, you will need to trim the ends. First, determine how tall you want the stook, and gradually cut the stems to that length. Then, you may need to snip the ends of stems, as shown, so the stook is balanced; keep tweaking it until you are satisfied.

TIP: Once you get the hang of this technique, you'll want to try it with everything. Any dried material with a fairly long stem can probably be used to make a stook. (You may also see these referred to as a sheaf.) Generally speaking, stooks are made from a single variety of flower, but artistic license prevailed in this project.

Herbal Guest Baskets

DESIGNERS: CORINNE KURZMANN & TERRY TAYLOR

Your visitors will be delighted to find this collection of aromatic gifts awaiting them. Decorate the sleek basket with a medallion of herbs and fill it with bath products to make your guests' stay especially enjoyable. These items are surprisingly easy to make, and you can find a variety of recipes if you want to make custom products for your visitors.

YOU WILL NEED

(FOR THE SOAP)

Soap or candy molds

Cooking spray

Paper towels

Clear glycerin melt-and-pour soap

Kitchen knife

Microwave-safe container

Microwave

Lavender

Soap colorant (optional)

Decorative papers and ribbons

(FOR THE FOOTBATH)

¼ cup (59 ml) table or sea salt

Dried herbs—rosemary, peppermint, and kelp

Glass or ceramic container

Mortar and pestle (optional)

Essential oil (optional)

Decorative bag

(FOR THE HERBAL BATH TEA)

Dried flowers and herbs—lavender, comfrey leaf, rose petals, and passionflower

Tea bag or muslin bag

(FOR THE BASKET DECORATION)

Chrome basket

Aluminum tooling foil

Large craft punch

Stylus

Mouse pad

Hot glue gun and glue sticks

1 To make the lavender soap, first spray the molds with a light coating of cooking spray, then wipe the mold with your fingers or a paper towel, as shown. Cut the soap into chunks and place it in the microwave-safe container. Follow the manufacturer's instructions for melting the soap; you can also melt the soap in a double boiler if you prefer.

2 Pour a thin layer of melted soap in the molds. Sprinkle in lavender flowers as shown; add colorant if you wish. Then, fill the soap molds with melted soap and allow the soaps to harden. Invert the molds and release the soaps. Wrap each soap with decorative paper and ribbon to create a pleasing presentation.

3 To blend the footbath, mix ¼ cup (59 ml) of salt and the desired amount of rosemary, peppermint, and kelp in a container. If you prefer a finer mix, use a mortar and pestle to grind the ingredients. You can add a few drops of essential oil for fragrance, if desired. Place the mixture in a decorative bag. To use, simply swirl into warm water.

5 To decorate the basket, punch out two medallions from the tooling foil. Use a stylus or other blunt object to emboss the front side of the medallion, as shown, working on a mouse pad to protect your surface. Place sprigs of lavender around the perimeter of the medallion and hot glue into place; then glue the two medallion pieces together. Affix to the basket with hot glue.

TIP: Contrary to common advice about dried flowers, encourage your visitors to leave this basket in the guest bathroom, as the humidity will release the aroma of the herbs in the medallion.

VARIATION

You can substitute most any of your favorite herbs in these recipes.

4 For the herbal bath tea, add lavender, comfrey leaf, rose petals, and passionflower until you have about ¼ to ⅓ cup (59 to 79 ml) of herbal mixture. Seal in a tea bag or place in a muslin bag. To use, place the bag of herbs in 2 cups (473 ml) of boiling water, cover, and steep for 20 minutes. Then, add the infusion to the bath.

Natural Table Runner

DESIGNER: BARBARA ZARETSKY

This exquisite tableau of twigs, flowers, and herb blossoms form a stunning natural table runner. Let spontaneity guide you when you create this decoration, and be willing to adapt your design as you proceed. Consider the surface of your table, your linens, and your glassware when you choose the floral materials. Here, the yarrow and the gold-rimmed glasses complement each other perfectly.

YOU WILL NEED

6 birch twigs

Scissors or floral snips

2 bunches of yarrow

2 bunches of Australian daisy

2 bunches of lavender

1 stalk of hydrangea

1 Set your table first, putting plates, silverware, glassware, and linens on the table as you prefer. In this design, clear salad plates were placed atop the linens and dinner plates for a clean, contemporary feel. Begin with the longest elements of the table runner, the birch twigs. Arrange as desired; clip to the appropriate length, if needed. Remember that you may want to adjust the size of your materials, as well as the arrangement, while you are working.

2 Add the yarrow, as in the photo above right, trying to array the materials naturally and casually. Next, add some bunches of Australian daisy, clipping the stems as desired and filling out the arrangement. Now, place the lavender under the flowers, perpendicular to the flow of the twigs.

3 To complete the table runner, add more yarrow as desired. Tweak the design as necessary, and then add some hydrangea for the centerpiece; use scissors, snips, or your fingers to remove pieces of hydrangea from the stalk as needed. Finally, cut or break off some small florets of hydrangea and distribute them around the table as desired.

Curtain with Pansy Streamers

DESIGNER: VALERIE SHRADER

This delicate curtain will remind you of spring all year 'round. The ribbon streamers can move with the breeze, so the flowers seem to float in the air. Though the construction of the curtain is simple, you could merely add the streamers to a ready-made sheer, if desired.

YOU WILL NEED

Tape measure

1 yard (.9 m) of sheer fabric

Scissors

Sewing machine

Thread

2 yards (1.8 m) of sheer ribbon, 3 inches (7.6 cm) wide

Pins

Seed pearls

Beading needle

Beading thread

Wax paper

10 pansies

Decoupage medium

Flat paintbrush

Fray retardant

Sewing needle

2 Cut out two pieces of sheer ribbon for the streamers, each the height of the curtain, plus ½ inch (1.3 cm). Pin the ribbon to the curtain, making sure that the streamers are straight. Baste into place, if desired. Then, stitch the lengths of ribbon to the curtain while you make a 3-inch (7.6 cm) casing at the top of the curtain, as shown. (If you cut the fabric so the selvage is at the top edge of the curtain, you won't need to machine hem the casing first.)

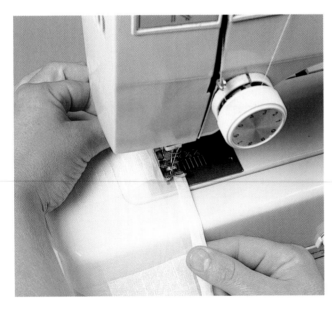

1 Measure the window where you plan to install the curtain. Then, cut out a piece of fabric sized to the dimensions of your window, plus 2 extra inches (5 cm) in width and 4 extra inches (10.2 cm) in height. Make a narrow machine hem around the sides and bottom of the sheer, as shown. Sharp sewing machine needles can make a big difference when you are sewing with lightweight fabric.

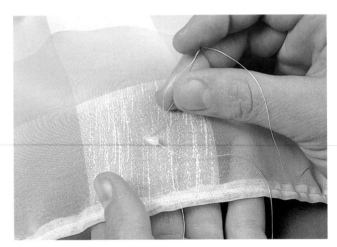

3 If desired, scatter seed pearls and attach with beading needle and thread. After you knot the thread to sew on each pearl, be sure to clip the tail completely, so it does not show through the curtain. If you want to embellish the curtain with pearls, be sure to do it at this stage, to avoid the possibility of damaging the flowers after they are added to the ribbon streamers.

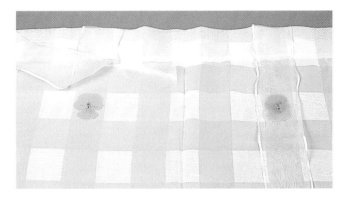

4 Place waxed paper between the curtain and the ribbon to protect the fabric. Plan to attach the pansies from the top down. Move the streamers out of the way while you decide where you want to place the pansies on the sheer, using the fabric underneath as a guide. The fabric used in this project made it easy to place the pansy in its proper place, with its distinct intersections of patterns; you may need to mark the spot where you plan to place the flowers, depending upon your fabric selection.

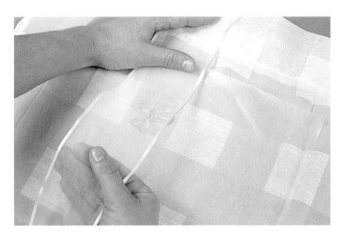

5 With a flat paintbrush, apply decoupage medium to the front of the flower, working from the middle out. Make sure that the entire surface of the pansy is covered with a thin coat of the medium. Place the pansy on the wax paper, face up, and use the wax paper to manipulate the flower into the proper position, if necessary. Then, gently place the ribbon on top of the pansy, as shown, and put a piece of wax paper on top of the streamer as you press the flower with your fingers, working from the inside out. Use wax paper to blot up any excess decoupage.

Continue in this manner and attach pansies as desired, alternating each streamer. Allow to dry completely on the waxed paper.

6 Use the fray retardant on the edge of the ribbon and allow to dry. Then, turn the ribbon under and tack invisibly onto the hem of the curtain, catching only the back of the hem. Add the final pearl details if desired, one at the top of the ribbon and one at the bottom, to secure the streamer onto the curtain.

TIPS: You may need more fabric and ribbon than is listed here, depending upon the size of your window. Be sure to measure it before you purchase any material. When you are applying the decoupage medium to the pansies, try to coat the entire surface to achieve an even finish when the flowers dry. Don't use too much decoupage, however, or it may bleed through onto the curtain. Experiment with this technique before you begin your final project.

VARIATION

Make the ribbon streamers and attach them to an existing curtain. Delete the final seed pearls in step 6 if you prefer a free-flowing sheer; your streamer will really dance with the wind with this construction.

Pavé Rose Basket

DESIGNER: ALLISON SMITH

In the language of flowers, white roses mean love, respect, and beauty, and this elegant project speaks to all of those emotions. Use a pale and subtle approach like this one, or search for materials that are a bit more dramatic to effect a bolder color scheme. The flowing silk ribbons are the perfect final touch.

YOU WILL NEED

Kitchen knife

Block of floral foam

Metal hanging basket

2 dozen white roses

Floral preservative (optional)

Metal primer

Paintbrushes

Small containers

Pale pink paint

Crackle medium

Off-white outdoor acrylic paint

1 yard (.9 m) of hand-dyed bias-cut silk ribbon, 2¾ inches (6.9 cm) wide

Scissors

Fray retardant

1 yard (.9 m) of hand-dyed bias-cut silk ribbon, ½ inch (1.3 cm) wide

Buttons

Hot glue gun and glue sticks

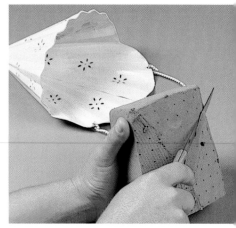

1 Using the kitchen knife, cut the floral foam to the shape of the basket. Make it just a little bit smaller than the container itself, to allow room to arrange the roses within the basket. Remove the foam from the basket and set it aside. Spray the roses with preservative, if desired.

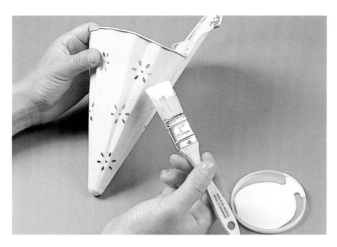

2 Prime the basket and allow it to dry. Paint with the pale pink paint and allow to dry; next, paint the basket with a thin coat of the crackle medium and allow it to dry for 20 to 30 minutes. Work quickly while you apply a thin coat of the off-white paint, as shown; paint it on with smooth, even strokes, being careful not to paint over areas that have already been covered. The crackle finish will develop as the paint dries. Let the basket dry completely.

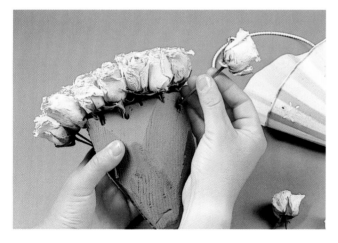

3 Snap the flower heads off the stems, leaving 3 to 4 inches (7.6 cm to 10.2 cm) of stem attached. Insert the flowers into the foam, packing them closely together. To create the pavé effect, make sure that the flowers are all at approximately the same height. Set the foam aside while you decorate the handle.

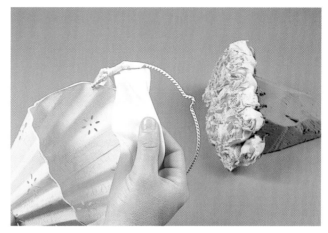

4 Attach the wide ribbon to one end of the handle by tying it in a knot, leaving about 8 inches (20.3 cm) extra hanging free on the side. Tightly wrap the ribbon around the handle. Tie the ribbon off on the other side, trim the ends, and treat with fray retardant.

5 Now, tightly wrap the narrow ribbon around the handle from end to end. Then, tie short lengths of the same ribbon to the handle. Hot glue the buttons onto the handle to disguise the knots.

TIP: The thickness of the coat of crackle medium will determine the size of the crackle on the finished product–a thin coat will produce a fine crackle, whereas a thick coat of crackle medium will produce a large crackle.

Wreath Triptych

DESIGNER: JOSENA AIELLO-BADER

Find a special place to display this stunning group of wreaths—on a mantel or shelf, perhaps? The differing hues of hydrangea unify the shades of the lavender and the larkspur, and the varied textures create visual interest. This basic idea can be translated into any color scheme that suits your mood.

YOU WILL NEED

(FOR ALL THREE WREATHS)

3 grapevine wreath forms, each
6 inches (15.2 cm) in diameter

Hot glue gun and 25 glue sticks

300 pieces of lavender

120 fern tips

3 yards (2.7 m) of light blue organdy ribbon

Scissors

Tape measure

30 stems of dark blue larkspur

5 medium heads of blue hydrangea

1 Since the lavender wreath is the most time consuming and demands the most material, it will be demonstrated here. Gather in your fingers a cluster of five to eight lavender heads, putting the tips mostly together. Cut off the stems at the ¾-inch (1.9 cm) length. Cover the ends with hot glue and lay them down on the wreath form.

2 Gather up another cluster of lavender flowers, and then lay the second group of flower heads onto the wreath so they cover the hot glue from the first cluster. Continue in this same manner until the wreath form is covered. Remember to glue the flower clusters to the outside and inside of the wreath as well, not just the front. Each cluster should be covering the hot glue from the previous one.

3 Once the wreath is covered with lavender and has a good shape, with even coverage and no gaps, hot glue the fern tips to the wreath. Again make clusters of two to three tips, and be sure to hot glue them down into the flower heads—don't just place them on top. Do this evenly on the front of the wreath as well as the inside and the outside of the form.

4 Cut 1 yard (.9 m) of ribbon and pull it through the grapevine on the back of the wreath form. Tie a knot above the wreath where you want to make the bow, first a full knot and then a two-loop bow. Then, trim off the extra ribbon.

FOR THE ADDITIONAL WREATHS

Use the same basic method to make all the wreaths, but there are a few special considerations for the remaining two. To create the larkspur wreath, at top right, you need to break the larkspur flower stems a few times to get clusters about the same size as the lavender. However, it is important that stems don't stick out of the clusters; they can be trimmed out once the clusters are hot glued onto the wreath form. Add the fern tips and ribbon as in steps 3 and 4.

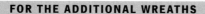

The hydrangea wreath, at lower right, is a quickie. Simply break apart the large flower heads into smaller sizes that are still held together by a stem. Cover the bottom of the flower bunches with hot glue and stick them onto the wreath form; bunch the flowers right next to each other so no grapevine shows. When you're happy with the shape of the wreath, add the fern tips and ribbon.

Sublime Stationery Set

DESIGNER: NICOLE TUGGLE

Make a special place for this portfolio on your desk. Like a flower, it's lovely yet delicate, so treat it gently; at the same time, it's very functional, keeping all of your letter writing needs together quite beautifully. Simply create more of the cards and the notepaper as needed, and enjoy this project for many seasons.

Thick decorative paper, 1 sheet cut to 10 x 17 inches (25.4 x 43.2 cm) and 1 sheet cut to 6 x 6 inches (15.2 x 15.2 cm)

Ruler

Pencil

Butter knife or bone folder

Clear-drying craft glue

Scissors

Small paintbrush

Foam brush

4 blank greeting cards, each 3½ x 5 inches (8.9 x 12.7 cm)

Gold decorative paper, 4 pieces cut to 2 x 3¾ inches (5 x 9.5 cm) and 1 piece cut to 2 x 5 inches (5 x 12.7 cm)

White decorative paper, 4 pieces cut to 1¾ x 3½ inches (4.4 x 8.9 cm) and 1 piece cut to 1½ x 4½ inches (3.8 x 11.4 cm)

8 pressed flowers

15 pieces of white paper, each 5 x 6½ inches (12.7 x 16.5 cm)

Awl

Large-gauge needle

Waxed linen or thick sewing thread

1 To make the stationery folder, take the large sheet of thick paper and lay it flat on the work surface. Measure and mark with a pencil ¼ inch (6 mm) from each edge. Fold each edge over and press down flat using a bone folder or the edge of a butter knife. Apply glue with the small paintbrush to glue each flap down, and let dry. With the paper lying with the long side toward you, mark the center point lightly with a pencil. Measure ½ inch (1.3 cm) out from that center point. Fold along these lines as shown to create the side spine of the folder.

2 To create the card pocket, put the smaller sheet of thick paper on the work surface. Measure, cut, and score the paper according to the template on page 79. Fold the top and bottom edges under ¼ inch (6 mm) and glue down; let dry. Fold the bottom flap and side flaps at the scored edges, and use the paintbrush to coat the surface with a thin layer of glue; then press together as shown, forming a pocket. Let dry.

3 Use the foam brush to coat the back of the pocket with a layer of glue. Then, position it at the center point of the left inside cover of the folder and press down, working along the surface of the pocket's flaps with your fingers. Use the butter knife or bone folder for support, as shown, and be careful not to crush the pocket. You want to keep its rectangular shape, with the sides flat.

4 Embellish the cards by gluing a piece of the 2 x 3¾-inch (5 x 9.5 cm) gold paper at the center point of the card. Press the paper down with your fingers to eliminate any bubbles. Glue a piece of the 1¾ x 3½-inch (4.4 x 8.9 cm) white paper directly on top of the gold paper. Use the small paintbrush to coat the back of a single pressed flower with a thin layer of glue, taking care to cover each petal and the center point, as shown. Place the flower down on the center point of the white paper and press down very carefully. Repeat for the remaining cards.

5 To make the writing pad, line up the sheets of white paper in a small stack. Mark a series of holes that are ½ inch (1.3 cm) from the top of the paper. First, mark one at the center point, and then one at each side; the latter should be ½ inch (1.3 cm) from the side as well as ½ inch (1.3 cm) from the top. Use the awl and carefully perforate each point, making holes that go through the entire stack of paper. Thread the needle and knot the end, leaving about a 1-inch (2.5 cm) tail. Starting at the back of the stack, sew through the center hole. Sew through the left hole to the back of the paper. Sew back up through the center hole and back through the right hole, as shown. Tie off at the center point with the tail of the thread, knot, and cut off any excess.

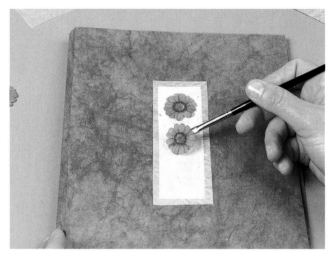

6 Hide the thread by covering the top edge of the writing pad with the decorative paper. Simply coat some paper with glue, wrap around the top edge, and cut off the excess from the sides. Let dry. Glue down a single pressed flower at the top center point. To attach to the folder, coat the back of the last page with a thin layer of glue. Center the pad over the right inside cover of the folder and press down, moving your fingers along the surface of that last sheet as shown, eliminating any bubbles and ensuring it is firmly attached. Let dry.

7 Embellish the cover of the folder by gluing down a piece of 2 x 5-inch (5 x 12.7 cm) gold decorative paper at the center point. Glue a piece of $1\frac{1}{2}$ x $4\frac{1}{2}$-inch (3.8 x 11.4 cm) white decorative paper on top. Finally, glue three pressed flowers down along the center point. Let dry.

TIP: To remove the notepaper, use a ruler or other straight implement as a guide and rip each sheet off carefully as you use it. Remember that you can easily replenish your supply of cards and notepaper.

First Blush of Spring Swag

DESIGNER: JOSENA AIELLO-BADER

Use some of the season's earliest blooming flowers to create this spectacular display. Although you'll need quite a bit of material for a project this size, it's very simple to dry your own daffodils by merely placing them upright in a vase. This basic design can be adapted to use the twigs or foliage of your choosing.

2 strands of wire, each 30 feet (9 m) long

Tape measure

Roll of brown waxed floral tape

Scissors

2 brown pipe cleaners

150 pussy willow tips

Pruners

75 daffodils

Hot glue gun and 25 hot glue sticks

90 to 100 fern tips

2 After the wire is wrapped, measure your window again to determine where to place the brown pipe cleaners. Make a loop in the wire, and then use a double half-hitch knot to attach one of the brown pipe cleaners near the end of the top of the swag. Add the other pipe cleaner in the same manner, as shown; place it at the bend where it will hang from the other side of the window. Hold it up again to check the placement, if necessary. Put the base down on a large working area near your hot glue gun.

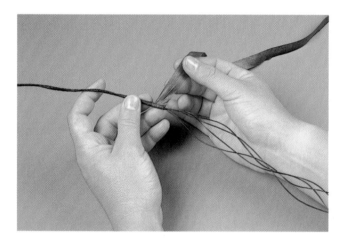

1 Fold the strands of wire in half to create a 15-foot-long (4.5 m) base. To plan the swag, measure the door or window you wish to decorate and note where you want to place the bend. Shape the wire base into a swag on your work surface. Then, using the brown waxed floral tape, start at either end and wrap the wire with the tape as shown; because the amount of wrapping can be somewhat challenging, you may find it more manageable to cut or tear the tape into 12- to 18-inch (30.5 to 45.7 cm) lengths for this step. It may be a little easier to stop wrapping at the corner and then begin again on the other side. Keep the tape tight as you wrap; stretching the tape makes the wax hold onto the wire. The tape gives the wire more body and prevents the material from slipping.

3 Trim the pussy willow into pieces 6 to 18 inches (15.2 to 45.7 cm) in length, in batches of four to six stems. Make a small bunch of four stems of varied lengths, and hold the stems onto the wire as you wrap the tape tightly around the pussy willow and the wire base, starting at the end of the wire. Be sure to use tips only, so there are no exposed stems. Take another bunch of stems of various lengths, trim the bottoms even, and place them on the wire base while you tightly wrap tape around the ends, as

shown. The tips of each successive bundle should cover the wrapped stem ends of the previous bundle, and so on. Continue until you reach the brown pipe cleaner at the bend in the swag.

4 When you have reached the pipe cleaner, start again at the other end of the base and proceed as before. Wrap as many little bundles of varied length pussy willow tips as it takes for you to meet at the bend. At the corner pipe cleaner you should have tape showing from both directions, as shown. If you need to disguise the ends of the wire base, you can loop them through and around the pussy willow branches.

5 Next, you'll make bundles of two and three daffodil blossoms and cut off most of the stems, leaving ½ to 1 inch (1.3 to 2.5 cm) remaining. Hot glue the stem ends and set on the garland, as shown, holding in place until the glue is cool. Keeping the daffodils short and close to the base is an effective design device because they appear heavy, while the

pussy willow is wispy; the flower heads can also hide the tape. Continue adding the daffodil clusters, keeping them close to the base. Neither the tape nor the hot glue should be visible in the finished product.

6 Add the fern tips to complete the project, again using only the tips so that no stems show. Use enough material to hide any of the hot glue that may be visible. Make sure that the fern and daffodils are evenly distributed in the swag. To install, hang the swag using the brown pipe cleaners.

TIP: You can usually harvest pussy willow in sunny locations where there is poorly drained soil, near rivers and creeks, but it shouldn't be taken without the landowner's permission. It's also available at florist shops.

SUBLIME STATIONERY SET TEMPLATE

page 71

CONTRIBUTING DESIGNERS

JOSENA AIELLO-BADER has been a professional floral designer for almost 20 years and her designs have appeared in many Lark books. She enjoys harvesting material and creating low-cost, yet lovely projects.

CORINNE KURZMANN leads an eclectic life in Asheville, North Carolina, with her husband Bob, 10 children, two hounds, one cat, and a large garden. She owns Diggin Art, a landscape and retail company.

SUSAN MCBRIDE is a graphic designer and multi-media artist. She is an avid gardener and animal lover. Susan, her husband, daughter, and pets live in Asheville, North Carolina.

JOAN K. MORRIS had a childhood interest in sewing that turned into professional costuming for motion pictures. She also ran her own clay wind chime business for 15 years. Since 1993, her Asheville, North Carolina coffeehouse, Vincent's Ear, has provided a vital meeting place for all varieties of artists and thinkers. Her work has appeared in *Beautiful Ribbon Crafts* and *Gifts for Baby*, both published in 2003 by Lark Books.

ALLISON SMITH has a home-based business specializing in providing deluxe tourist accommodations in remote locations in Western North Carolina. She is also an avid crafter and designer in addition to being a full-time mother. She has created projects for numerous Lark books, including *Decorating Baskets* (2002), *Girls' World* (2002), and *Decorating Candles* (2001). She lives in Asheville, North Carolina.

TERRY TAYLOR is a mixed media artist whose work has been shown in numerous exhibitions. He is the full-time craft guru at Lark Books.

NICOLE TUGGLE'S recent work has focused on collage and assemblage constructions, but she is a mixed-media artist. She finds beauty in found objects and old, neglected treasures. See more of her work at http://www.sigilation.com.

BARBARA ZARETSKY, a textile and graphic designer, has been creating wearable textile art for over 15 years. Specializing in surface design and needlework, her designs have been featured in *Fiberarts* magazine and at boutiques, galleries, and craft shows. She studied textile design at Northern Illinois University and The Art Institute of Chicago.

ACKNOWLEDGMENTS

Thanks to the designers, a talented and diverse bunch of people, who created the projects for this book. A special mention should go to the professional floral designer in the group, Josena Aiello-Bader, whose generous advice was invaluable to me. Her colleagues at The Gardener's Cottage, in Asheville, North Carolina, were kind and giving of their time as well. I appreciated the cheerful enthusiasm of hand model Dietra Garden, a talented artist in her own right. And Marcianne Miller, your flower press changed my life. Maybe I'll give it back someday.

Thanks also to the people who made the book beautiful, photographer Keith Wright, his partner Wendy Wright, and art director Celia Naranjo. They did a wonderful job! Susan McBride and Michael Murphy were gracious hosts for the photo shoot; thank you for letting us borrow your lovely home and garden for a few days. I am grateful for the patience and advice of senior editor Deborah Morgenthal, who helped me during an extremely busy time.

Finally, I must express my sincere gratitude to project coordinator Terry Taylor, whose good humor, creativity, and warm heart were much appreciated during the production of this book. I couldn't have done it without you, Terry. Thank you.

INDEX

Arrangements: tonal arrangement, 37; stook, 56; table runner, 61; pavé basket, 66; wreath triptych, 68; swag, 75

Boxes, 49

Candles, 42
Coasters, 51
Crafting tips, 16–21
Curtain, 63

Design tips, 20–21
Drawer pulls, 24
Drying techniques: air, 11; silica gel, 11–12; microwave, 12

Floral centerpiece, 28
Flowers: choosing, 9; harvesting, 9–10; preparation for drying, 10; purchasing, 21–22; sealing, 14–15; storing, 15
Frame, 42

Gift bags, 30
Guest baskets, 58

Lamps: translucent, 26; decorated, 35

Mirror, 53

Pressing techniques: book, 13; traditional flower press, 13–14; microwave flower press, 14

Sachet bag, 46
Shadow box, 39
Stationery set, 71

Tools and supplies: floral, 16; crafting, 17
Trellis, 33